VOLLEYBALL
THE SERVE

ZACHARY A. KELLY

The Rourke Corporation, Inc.
Vero Beach, Florida 32964

PHOTO CREDITS:
All photos © Tony Gray except © East Coast Studios: pages 4, 8

PROJECT EDITORS:
Harold Lockheimer
Connie Denaburg

EDITORIAL SERVICES:
Penworthy Learning Systems

Library of Congress Cataloging-in-Publication Data

Kelly, Zachary A., 1970-
   Volleyball—the serve / Zachary A. Kelly.
     p. cm. — (Volleyball)
   Includes index.
   ISBN 0-86593-507-6
   1. Volleyball—Serve. I. Title II. Series:
Kelly, Zachary A., 1970- Volleyball.
GV1015.5.S47K45 1998
796.325—dc21
                                           98–20630
                                               CIP
                                               AC

TABLE OF CONTENTS

SERVICE AREA

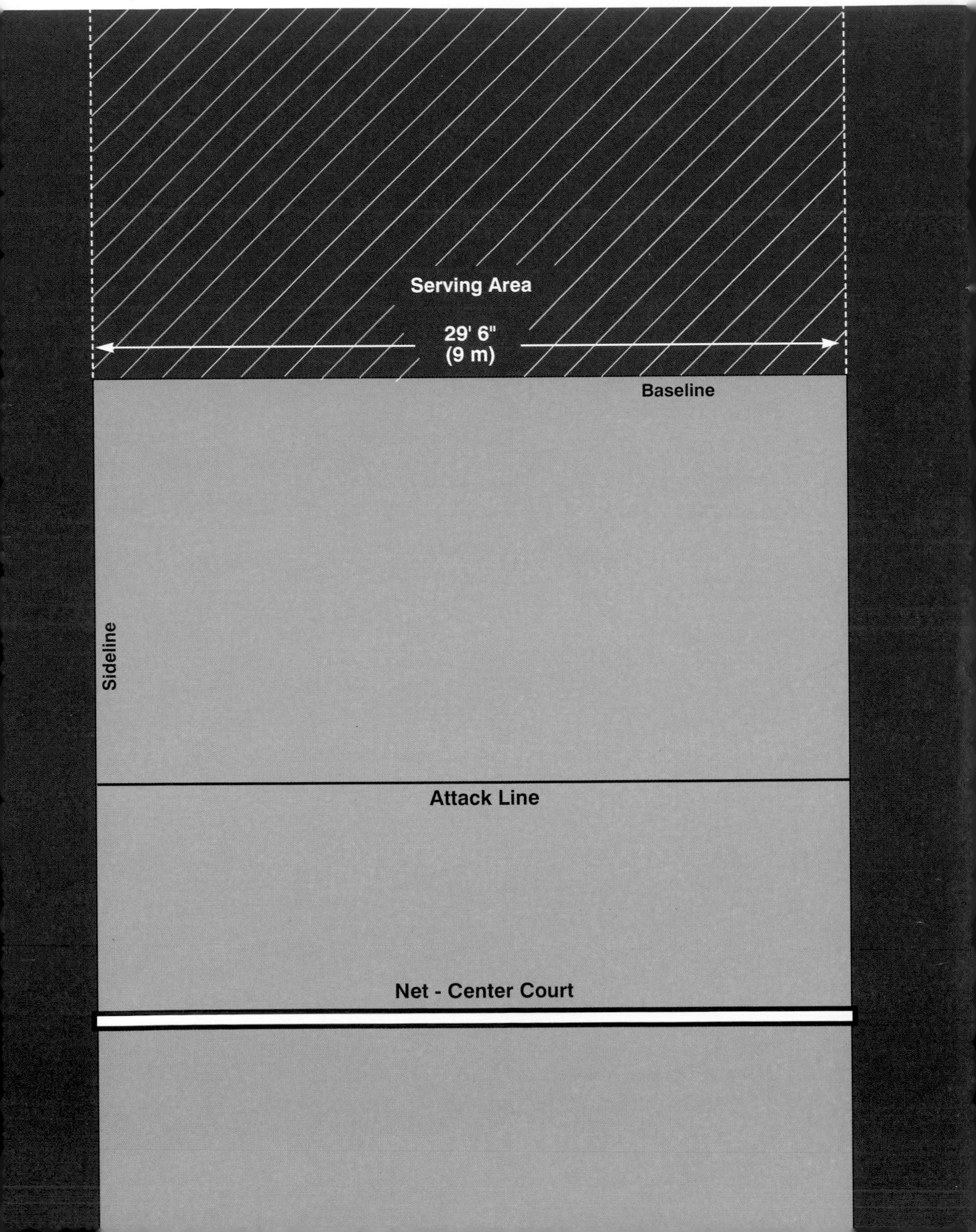

Serving Area

29' 6"
(9 m)

Baseline

Sideline

Attack Line

Net - Center Court

CHAPTER ONE

THE SERVE

The **serve** is one of the most important actions in volleyball. It is a way of putting the ball into play. To serve the ball, a server stands at the back of the court, tosses the ball up, and then hits it across the net to the other side of the court. The serve is the only play in volleyball in which the player has complete control. With practice, you can turn a serve into a powerful offensive weapon.

Every time a player serves, he or she has two goals. First, the server wants to hit a fair ball into the opposing team's court. Second, the server wants to make the serve difficult for the other team to receive. To be fair, the ball has to clear the net (without touching it) and land within the sidelines and baseline of the other team's court. This kind of accuracy takes practice. Once a player can hit fair balls every time he or she serves, it is time to practice more challenging serves.

There are a variety of different serves. You should learn and practice each one so you can become a more effective server for your team.

Service and Rotation

The serve is important to the structure of the game. Not only does the serve begin every rally; but when the service changes, the players **rotate** their positions.

Every volley starts with a serve, including the first one in the game. To choose which team may serve first, the two teams toss a coin. Once the ball is in play, the team that serves continues serving until it loses a rally. Only the serving team can earn points. When the serving team loses a rally, the other team earns the right to serve. This turn is called a **side-out**.

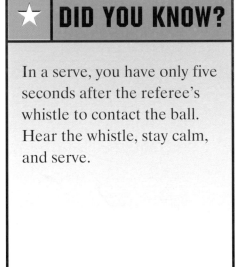

★ **DID YOU KNOW?**

In a serve, you have only five seconds after the referee's whistle to contact the ball. Hear the whistle, stay calm, and serve.

Connecting with the ball at the right height is an important skill.

SIMPLE CLOCKWISE ROTATION

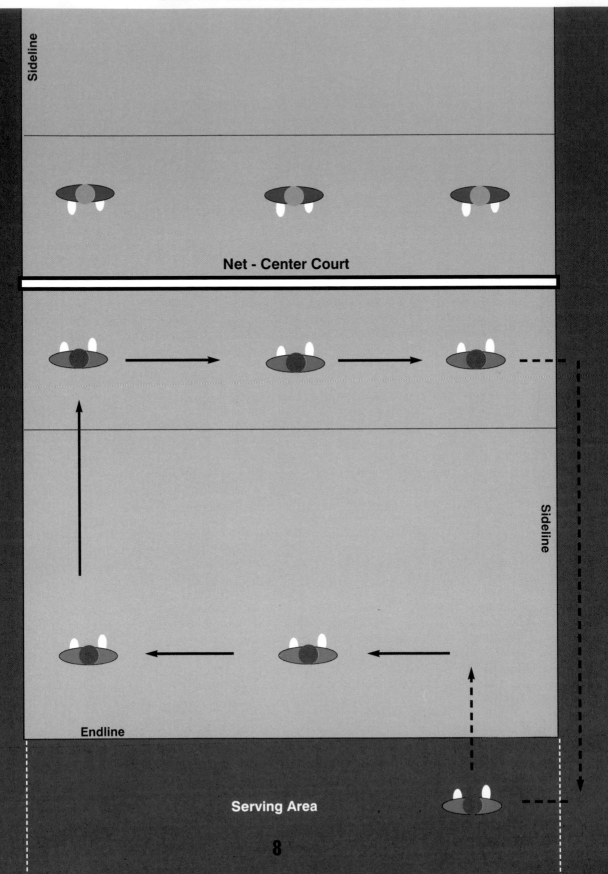

Sideline

Net - Center Court

Sideline

Endline

Serving Area

When a team earns a side-out, players must rotate positions before they begin service. That means each player moves one position clockwise until the next side-out on their side. After a serve players may switch positions. **Front** and **back court** positions have different rules to follow, so it is important for a player to know every position well. All players must be in their new positions before the team's server begins serving the ball. If not, this is called an overlap and a point or side-out is awarded.

Rules about the Serve

Before the serve, players on both sides of the net must be in position. A back court player cannot be in front of a front court player, and the positions may not overlap side to side or front to back. The server must stay in the serving area behind the baseline until the ball is in play. That means a server cannot cross the end line or step onto the court until he or she has served the ball.

During the serve, the server stays in the serving area and hits the ball over the net onto the other team's court. Remember, the ball is fair if it does not touch the net and if it is within the sidelines and end lines.

DID YOU KNOW?

USA Volleyball is the organization in charge of the U.S. Men's and Women's Olympic Teams. They also govern junior and adult volleyball play.

No other member of the server's team can touch the ball until it has crossed the net.

After service, players may move to any position, though they still must follow the rules of their positions. If the serving team wins the volley, they win a point. If the other team wins the volley, it earns a side-out.

Tips for Any Serve

Most good volleyball players focus on details to improve their serves. For every serve, they use similar motions. This keeps their plan for the serve hidden from the other team until the other team receives it.

Practicing foot placement helps with your serve.

Follow-through adds control to any style of serve.

Advanced players will sometimes look to the left side of the court but serve to the right. This is to fool the opponents who are taught to watch the server's eyes in hope of predicting where the ball might go. Most players also pay attention to their feet. Keeping a wide step between them gives good support. For balance and power, a server will put forward the opposite foot from the serving arm.

Another detail most volleyball players work on is follow-through. Follow-through is the movement a server makes after he or she hits the ball, which completes a serve. Follow-through lets a player put the full force of his or her body behind the ball. Good follow-through also helps a server control the ball. Players also focus on the ball from the beginning of the serve until the ball is contacted. This concentration is very important to a good serve and assurance that the ball will hit its target on the other side of the net.

THE UNDERHAND AND OVERHAND FLOATER

The Underhand Floater

The first serve most players learn is the **underhand floater**. The underhand floater is a serve in which a player releases the ball with the non-hitting hand just as the hitting hand swings up from underneath. It is the easiest serve to learn, and most players use it until every serve they make is nearly perfect. The name "floater" refers to how the ball looks in the air. Since this serve puts no **spin** on the ball, the ball wobbles as it travels.

A ball without spin is not stable and seems to float through the air like a bubble. A spinning ball is more stable.

The underhand serve is easy to learn and easy to hit, but it is also easy for the other team to receive. The underhand floater is usually slow and travels high. A ball that goes high gives the other team more time to prepare their defense. Most players use the underhand floater as a beginning serve and add other serves as soon as possible.

Making the Serve

To begin an underhand floater serve, stand with the foot of your hitting side a large step behind the other foot. Your toes, knees, hips, and shoulders should face the direction in which you will serve the ball. Your weight should be evenly distributed. Hold the ball at waist level in front of your body with your non-hitting hand.

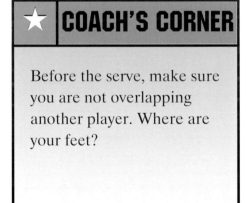

★ COACH'S CORNER

Before the serve, make sure you are not overlapping another player. Where are your feet?

This player shows the perfect starting position for an underhand serve.

Body form is important throughout a serve.

Swing your hitting arm straight back behind your body. Shift your weight from your back foot to your front foot as you swing your arm forward. Release the ball from your non-hitting hand right before your hitting hand contacts the ball. Contact with the ball should be with a firm open palm. Remember to keep your eyes on the ball ALL the time.

After you contact the ball, finish the swing of your hitting hand. This follow-through will make sure the ball has maximum power behind it and will give you control of its path. Now step onto the court to defend your area.

The Overhand Floater

Overhand serves are more difficult to perform but offer more power. In the **overhand floater**, a player tosses the ball up and hits it over the net with little or no spin. There are two differences between the underhand and overhand floater serves. In the underhand floater, the server hits the ball underneath. In an overhand floater, the server hits the ball through the middle, punching it over the net, avoiding an aggressive follow-through.

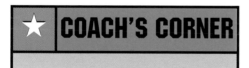

COACH'S CORNER

Underhand serves are great beginning serves. Make sure you toss the ball before you contact it.

The other difference is the height of the hit. The player contacts the ball at waist height in an underhand serve. In an overhand service, the hit is nearly head high.

An overhead floater is the more difficult for the other team to receive. It takes a lower path and moves much quicker, which does not give the opposing team much time to react. It is also a floater serve, which means it wobbles and wiggles as it crosses the net. These two factors make the overhand a challenging serve to receive. As you perfect this serve you can learn how to make variations that will cause the ball to react differently with each method.

This player shows how to begin an overhand serve.

Keep your eye on the ball when performing a serve.

Making the Serve

The key to a good overhand floater is the toss of the ball. It should have no spin and sufficient height.

To do the overhand floater, begin with your feet apart as for the underhand floater. Put the foot opposite your hitting arm in front. Keep your toes, hips, and shoulders facing the direction you want the ball to travel. Your weight should be evenly distributed. Hold the ball at shoulder level as you begin the serve.

Toss the ball up in front of your hitting shoulder. Put your hitting arm back with your elbow high and your open hand near your ear. Shift your weight forward as you move to hit the ball. Drive your elbow forward, keeping your arm straight, and hit the ball in the middle with the heel of your hand, using a quick snap of the wrist. Remember to watch the ball ALL the time.

After hitting the ball, your arm should stop moving, like a punch. It should look like a throw that stops short. Let your weight continue to move onto your other foot, drop your arm, and move onto the court.

CHAPTER THREE

THE TOPSPIN AND ROUNDHOUSE FLOATER

The Topspin

The **topspin** serve is more difficult to perform than either of the floater serves. To perform a topspin serve, the player tosses the ball up about three feet (about one meter) above the shoulders and hits the ball near head height. When the open hand contacts the ball, the player snaps the wrist forward, giving the serve a spin. A topspin serve travels on a predictable path and drops quickly.

The spin on this serve keeps the ball on course. Normally this is a disadvantage to the serving team, but many times in a game the topspin is the best choice. Because the ball drops quickly, it is a good serve to use to throw off the other team's timing. Giving a topspin serve after several overhand floaters can surprise the other team. Many teams also use it when the other team is ready for a deep serve. The topspin serve drops quickly. If the other team is not ready for a shallow serve, they might miss this serve.

Making A Topspin Serve

Getting ready for a topspin serve looks like the overhand floater. Begin with your feet a stride apart. The foot on your non-hitting side should be in back, and your weight should fall on that foot. Aim your toes, hips, and shoulders in the direction you want to send the ball. Keep the ball at shoulder height and prepare to toss.

Toss the ball about three feet (about one meter) up and swing your hitting arm back. Your elbow should be high and your hand should be close to your ear. Shift your weight forward. Contact the ball with the heel of your open hand and your arm fully extended.

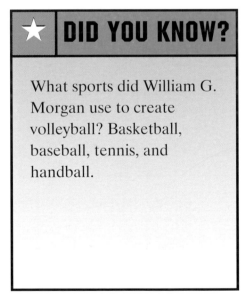

★ **DID YOU KNOW?**

What sports did William G. Morgan use to create volleyball? Basketball, baseball, tennis, and handball.

This player is in a good position for performing the topspin serve.

Practicing overhand serves again and again helps a player gain better control.

As you hit the ball, flex your wrist forward quickly to give the serve its spin. Your fingers should be spread to touch the ball as you flex your wrist. Keep your eye on the ball at all times.

All the movement of your arm should be from back to front. After contacting the ball, allow your arm to finish its swing, and drop it to your waist. Now, step onto the court.

The Roundhouse Floater

To serve a **roundhouse floater**, the server faces the sideline with the non-hitting side of the body closer to the net. The player tosses the ball up and swings the hitting-side hip, arm, and shoulder around to hit the ball much like an overhand floater. This serve uses several large muscle groups, giving it great power. A roundhouse floater is effective for putting the serve deep into the opponent's court. Some players use this serve as a standard deep serve until they can master the overhand floater. In this serve, the player begins with an obvious stance. That can be a disadvantage when you are trying to keep the other team from guessing your plan.

DID YOU KNOW?

Several sportswear companies, including Nike, Asics, Reebok, and Kaepa make shoes specifically for volleyball.

The roundhouse floater has more force behind it than other serves. It also uses the floater technique, making it a challenging serve to receive. Using the roundhouse floater between other serves can mess up the other team's timing, even if they see it coming.

Making a Roundhouse Serve

To serve a roundhouse floater, stand with your feet a comfortable stride apart, the foot of your non-hitting side forward. The toe, knee, hip and shoulder of the non-hitting side should face the direction you are serving the ball. Your hitting side faces away from the ball.

Learning how to receive a roundhouse floater serve takes practice.

The beginning stance for the roundhouse floater serve is similar to the topspin.

You are standing correctly if you are facing the sideline. Put your weight on your back foot and hold the ball in front of you, waist high.

Toss the ball about three feet (about one meter) up in front of your hitting shoulder. With your hitting arm fully extended, drop it back behind you and swing it over your head. Shift your weight forward as you swing your arm, and turn your hitting side toward the ball. Hit the ball directly in front of your body with the heel of your open hand. Keep your wrist locked and punch the ball as in an overhand floater. As you hit the ball, your hitting-side toe, knee, hip, and shoulder should be facing it.

The arm motion of the hit should stop with contact. After the hit, drop your arm to your side and move onto the court.

CHAPTER FOUR

THE JUMP SERVE AND OTHER ADVANCED SERVES

The Jump Serve

The **jump serve** is more advanced than any of the four serves already discussed in this book. It is not a technique for beginners. In a jump serve, the player tosses the ball up and jumps to meet the ball. The server hits the ball with a fully extended arm while at the highest point of the jump. Most people consider this the most complex serve in volleyball.

The jump serve is similar to a **spike**. (The spike is a powerful offensive technique that requires a player to hit the ball while he or she is in the air.) Before hitting the ball, a player must toss it up and take several steps. Then the player takes off and jumps to meet the ball in the air. This approach gives a fast, powerful serve that is difficult for the other team to receive. However, it is also a very difficult serve to perform. A player should begin using the jump serve only after becoming an expert on all other serves and after getting advice from a coach.

Making a Jump Serve

The first step in the jump serve is preparing the approach. Begin several steps behind the end line with your feet a comfortable distance apart and your toes, knees, hips, and shoulders facing the direction of your serve. Toss the ball up using your hitting hand, non-hitting hand, or both hands, whichever gives you the most control. Toss it so that if it were hit, the ball would land just inside the court. Keep your eyes on the ball.

★ **DID YOU KNOW?**

In 1916 in the Philippine Islands, the set and spike were introduced to the sport.

Practice jumping and hitting the ball to help both your jump serve and spike.

Keeping your arm straight during a jump serve is important for ball control and power.

Now begin your approach. Take a large step with the foot on your non-hitting side. Then plant your hitting-side foot slightly ahead of the other. Plant your other foot next to it and jump. As you plant your feet, extend your arms straight behind you. At the jump, swing your hitting arm back with your hand near your ear and elbow high. Swing your other arm forward naturally.

At the highest point of the jump, hit the ball with your arm fully extended. The heel of your open hand should hit the ball's middle. Let your fingers wrap around the ball and flex your wrist sharply to create a spin. Finish your hit with full arm follow-through. Then, cushion your landing by bending your knees slightly and step onto the court.

Body Position

Advanced players continue improving their serve by watching several factors. One of these factors is body position. Position includes eye focus, even motions, foot placement, and follow-through.

Keep your eyes on the ball for control and accuracy. Although it may seem easy to remember, keeping your eyes on the ball throughout a serve takes practice.

★ DID YOU KNOW?

In the 1992 Olympics, both the men's and women's volleyball teams won the bronze medal.

Even motions make consistent (same each time) serves. Keep your movements as similar as possible each time you serve. This will keep the other team from guessing your strategy and help make each serve a good one.

The position of your feet determines your stability. Keep them wide enough apart for good support. Shifting your weight from the back foot to the front as you serve gives you power and balance. Following-through lets you hit the ball when your arm is at the center of the arc it makes during a serve. This way you transfer the most power from your hand to the ball.

Coaches often show their players proper techniques.

An important part of every serve is how you contact (hit) the ball.

Spin and Accuracy

If a player knows how to put spin on the ball, he or she can control the serve better. A ball spins away from pressure. If hit on the left, it will spin to the right. If hit near the bottom, it will spin upward. In volleyball, the hit is usually up and to the left, to the right, or in the middle. (The underhand floater serve is hit directly underneath, not giving any spin.) If a player can master the spin, that player can serve an unexpected spin, or use a certain spin with a weak receiver.

To aim the ball, the server looks at the target, then looks only at the ball during the serve, aiming at that spot. Many coaches recommend practicing with a partner on the other side of the net, increasing the distance between you and the target. Putting a large X on a wall and increasing distance as you practice your aim is another good exercise for accuracy.

CHAPTER FIVE

CHOOSING A SERVE

Consistency

Consistency means making every serve with the same accuracy and control. Consistency alone can cause a team to win or lose a game. As you begin serving in a game, use only the serves you can make consistently. At first you may have only one serve to use. That's okay. Consistent service is better than varied service that is not consistent.

Learn new serves in the order of difficulty, beginning with the underhand floater. Your coach is the best person to help you do the harder serves when the time is right.

Being consistent on the court looks like you do the same thing over and over. Using the same technique every time you serve helps consistency. And it keeps the other team from knowing how you will serve until you do it. Even if you use different serves, keep your movements as similar as possible. Consistency is your greatest tool to turn a serve into an offensive weapon. Studying how advanced players serve may help, too.

Choosing Your Serve

So, which serve is best? The answer, of course, depends on the server's skills and the game situation. A serve is never a good choice if the server cannot do it consistently.

The First Serve

In a service, a player often has to serve the ball more than once. Sometimes, though, one serve may be the only chance you will get. In either case, the first serve is key.

That first serve must be accurate. The ball must clear the net and land fairly in the other team's court, even if the serve is easy to receive.

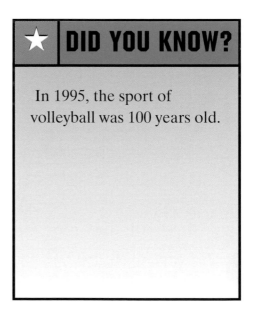

★ **DID YOU KNOW?**

In 1995, the sport of volleyball was 100 years old.

Tossing the ball to the right height for a serve is important.

A complex overhand serve is used only by skilled players.

A perfectly accurate first serve is important because it can turn the game to your team's control, giving you an advantage. If the first serve is not accurate, the team does not get a chance to score points.

For an accurate first serve, many players choose a simple serve to open the match. The second serve should be more difficult to receive, and the serves should grow more difficult as you continue serving. But—keep them consistent!

After the First Serve

Underhand floaters are good serves to use when you begin playing volleyball. As you learn other serves, you might use the underhand sometimes to throw off the other team's timing when they are expecting another kind of serve.

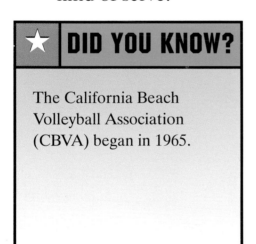

★ **DID YOU KNOW?**

The California Beach Volleyball Association (CBVA) began in 1965.

Overhand floaters are basic serves. The overhand floater travels faster and straighter than the underhand floater, giving the other team less time to react. Along with its unsteady flight, this straight path often makes the overhand floater a good choice.

Topspin serves travel fast and drop quickly. Use them in the middle of other serves to throw off the other team's timing. Since they are shallow serves, they are also good to serve to a team in a deep-court position.

A roundhouse floater looks different to the other team, which gives it away. Still, players sometimes use a roundhouse instead of an overhand floater because of its power. Most players do not use the jump serve until they are very experienced.

Where to Aim the Ball

Before you begin your serve, you need to know where you are sending the ball. How do you decide?

A really good serve is one the other team can't return.

Aiming your serve to different areas will keep your opponents guessing.

Keep in mind that you don't want the other team to receive your serve. Make your serves different from what they might expect. Don't give them too much time to receive. And play to their weak points, not to their strengths.

First, keep your serve unpredictable (for the other team). Change your target often to keep the other team guessing where you will aim the ball next.

If possible, cut short the other team's time for receiving. Give them less time to prepare by using low, fast serves. A **down-the-line serve** (which stays within a few feet of the sideline as it travels) will reach the other side fastest.

If the other team's formation shows that they are ready for a deep serve, aim shallow. Serving to the middle of the back court can be a good move. When in formation for your serve, the other team's players may be unable to communicate well. Therefore, they may be unable to receive such a serve.

Serve to weak passing players. If a new player or a substitute is on court, serve to that person. Weak passers and new players are more likely than their teammates to make mistakes.

GLOSSARY

backcourt (BAK KAWRT) — the area of the court between the attack line and the baseline

down-the-line serve (DOUN-thuh-LYN SERV) — a serve directed down the right sideline of the opposing teams' court

jump serve (JUMP SERV) — a difficult serve in which the player jumps up to meet the ball when serving

front court (FRUNT KAWRT) — area of the court between the net and the attack line

overhand floater (O ver HAND FLO ter) — a more advanced serve, performed with an overhand motion

rotate (RO tayt) — the movement of players through different positions during a game

roundhouse floater (ROUND HOUS FLO ter) — an advanced overhand serve using body weight to add force to the ball

serve (SERV) — the first hit of the ball over the net to begin a volley

sideout (SYD OUT) — a turnover of the ball from the serving to the receiving team in which no points are scored

GLOSSARY

spike (SPYK) — the attack move, performed by hitting the ball overhand over the net with a downward path

spin (SPIN) — a spinning motion put on the ball by hitting it a certain way

topspin serve (TAHP SPIN SERV) — a difficult serve using an upward thrust of the hand to cause the ball to spin while travelling over the net

underhand floater (UN der HAND FLO ter) — the basic volleyball serve, performed with an underhand motion

FURTHER READING

Find out more with these helpful books and information sites:

American Coaching Effectiveness Program, Rookie Coaches Volleyball Guide. Champagne, IL: Human Kinetics, 1993.

Fraser, Stephen D. *Strategies for Competitive Volleyball.* New York: Leisure, 1988.

Howard, Robert E. *An Understanding of the Fundamental Techniques of Volleyball.* Needham Heights, MA: Allyn and Bacon, 1996.

Kluka, Darlene, and Dunn, Peter. *Volleyball.* Wm. C. Brown, 1996.

Neville, William S. *Coaching Volleyball Successfully.* New York: Leisure, 1990.

Vierra, Barbara, and Ferguson, Bonnie Jill. *Volleyball: Steps to Success.* Human Kinetics, 1996.

American Volleyball Coaches Association at http://www.volleyball.org/avca/index.html

Complete worldwide source for volleyball information at http://www.volleyball.org/
This site includes descriptions and ordering information for many new books and videos; also, many links.

Great links: http://users.aol.com/vballusa/index.htm

Online Volleyball Magazine subscription page at http://www.volleyballmag.com/sub.htm

More volleyball information at http://www.volleyball.com

INDEX